Getting started journaling isn't something that you need to think about too hard. Yes, there are numerous types and styles of journals and ways to do this that may or may not be more effective depending on your goals, but you can simply get some paper (or your computer) and get started today.

- Dust Off Your Pen and Paper – You don't need anything special to keep a journal; in fact, purists believe that using pen and paper is the best way to journal because you can carry it with you anywhere and you don't need technology. So, there will be no excuses.

- Do It First Thing in the Morning – Don't procrastinate about keeping your journal. It's best to do it in the morning before you begin your day so that you have the right frame of mind for the day. Plus, you only need five to ten minutes, so it's not that big of a deal.

- Write Every Single Day – Whenever you choose to do it, try to set it up so that it becomes a ritual and a habit. Journaling every single day is going to be more effective than just doing it when you feel like it.

- Start Simply – Don't start being worried about style and substance right now; just work on the daily habit with pen and paper (or if it's easier for you, a computer or smartphone). Don't make it hard - just get going.

- Begin with Today – Start right now and write about your day today. That's the easiest thing to do. What of significance happened today? How did you feel about it? What would you do differently? What would you do the same?

- Try Different Types of Journals – Once you develop the habit, you can start trying different types of journaling like a bullet journal, or a vision journal, or maybe even a project journal for your next project.

Achieving Goals with Journaling

Journaling can help you achieve your goals because it will force you to think about them, consider the why and how, and delve deeper into the situation so that you can examine all sides of it. Read on to find out how journaling can help.

- It Forces You to Write Down Your Goals – When you start a journal, it basically is a way to force yourself to document your goals. Whether you write them down on paper or you use technology to get it all down doesn't matter. Once they're written, they are ready to tackle.

- It Makes You Consider Why and How – As you enter data into your journal, you'll be forced to face the why and how of your goal. This is especially true if you write down a goal and focus on it in your journal.

- It Enables You to Examine the Opportunities and Threats – When you are focused on goal making with your journal, you'll also explore opportunities and threats coming your way due to your goals. It helps you avoid roadblocks in advance.

- It Makes You Develop Steps for Success Based on Your Goals – When you see it written down, you'll want to notice and pull out any steps you've developed in your journal and put them in your calendar for scheduling.

- It Helps You Improve Goal Setting and Achievement – Each time you intentionally set goals, define steps to achieve the goals, and perform them, you are setting yourself up for being able to improve your skills.

- It Provides Accountability – Even if no one else is reading your journal, a private journal can help you become accountable to yourself. If you develop the habit of looking at your journal each day and put something else in there each day, it'll work great for helping you become more accountable.

- It Provides a Permanent Record – Having a permanent record of the things you've done in your life, whether it's personal or work, is a beautiful thing. Hardly anyone has a perfect memory, so you'll maintain the lessons learned better with the record to look back at.

- It May Be Inspirational – Depending on the journal, you might even be able to take the information inside and compile it into a real book for others to read to inspire them. You might also take from it steps for your success for a project and turn it into a course to inspire someone else.

Journaling is an excellent way to work toward achieving all your goals. It will even help you make better goals because the process of entering facts in your journal will cause you to see them in a more logical way that is more useful.

The Importance of Journaling

Keeping any type of journal will help with improving any mental health issues. However, if you really want to tackle a specific problem you're having, it will help to determine the right type of journal to keep. Keeping a particular kind of journal may work best for your issue.

- Boosts Your Mood – If you really want to boost your mood, keeping a gratitude journal is where it's at. All you have to do is once a day, preferably before bed, write down what you're grateful for today. It might not seem like much but it's very powerful for going to sleep, thinking positively about your life.

- Increases Your Sense of Well-Being – As you write out your thoughts, you'll start seeing issues from a new angle just because you're opening your mind to think about it. This is going to make you feel more capable of dealing with whatever happens.

- Lessens Symptoms of Depression – Understand that depression is something different from sadness, and that you likely need a counselor. Writing it all down can make it seem less horrific so that you can feel better. Plus, you can look back at days you thought life was "over" and see better days after.

- Lowers Avoidance Behaviors – Many people who have mental health issues practice avoidance behaviors such as not going to places that cause them anxiety, or not doing the things they need to do due to how they feel. When you write it out, it helps you get the feelings out but do the thing anyway.

- You'll Sleep Better – Pouring your heart out into a journal is a great way to get things off your chest. However, for sleep, go to the gratitude journal and write down what you're thankful for today and go to sleep thinking of that.

- Improves Your Memory – This is almost a situation where you want to say "duh" but it has to be said. Writing down things helps you remember them because you can go back and read it, but also because the act of writing something down enables you to recall it.

STAY POSITIVE AND HAPPY.
WORK HARD AND DON'T GIVE
UP HOPE.

BE OPEN TO CRITICISM AND KEEP LEARNING.

SURROUND YOURSELF WITH
HAPPY, WARM AND GENUINE
PEOPLE.

TENA DESAE

When do you feel the most hopeful? Who are you around when you feel this way?

_____

_____

_____

_____

_____

_____

_____

_____

_____

_____

_____

_____

_____

_____

_____

_____

_____

Be thankful for what you have; you'll end up having more. If you concentrate on what you don't have, you will never, ever have enough.

-- Oprah Winfrey

Let's celebrate your accomplishments today! How did you overcome a recent hardship? How long did you celebrate your victory?

_____

_____

_____

_____

_____

_____

_____

_____

_____

_____

_____

_____

_____

_____

_____

_____

_____

Do you want to be always happy?
Then give up fighting
for **negativity**
And learn the beautiful art
Of self-encouragement.

Sri Chinmoy

Mood swings are a common symptom of depression. When do you experience mood changes? Do people or things trigger your mood swings? How do you cope with changes in your mood?

_____

_____

_____

_____

_____

_____

_____

_____

_____

_____

_____

_____

_____

_____

_____

_____

_____

_____

Steps to a daily mindfulness practice.

- Find a quiet space. Using a cushion or chair, sit-up straight but not stiff; allow your head and shoulders to rest comfortably; place your hands on the tops of your legs with upper arms at your side.

- Close your eyes, take a deep breath, and   relax. Feel the fall and rise of your chest and the expansion and contraction of your belly. With each breath notice the coolness as it enters and the warmth as it exits. Don't control the breath but follow its natural flow.

Liz Mineo-Harvard Gazette

My favorite way to spend my day is...

_____

_____

_____

_____

_____

_____

_____

_____

_____

_____

_____

_____

_____

_____

_____

_____

Steps to a
daily mindfulness practice.

- Thoughts will try to pull your attention away from the breath. Notice them, but don't pass judgment. Gently return your focus to your breath. Some people count their breaths as a way to stay focused.

- A daily practice will provide the most benefits. It can be 10 minutes per day, however, 20 minutes twice a day is often recommended for maximum benefit.

Liz Mineo-Harvard Gazette

When will you incorporate mindfulness into your daily routine? What barriers do you think will appear when trying mindfulness ?

_____

_____

_____

_____

_____

_____

_____

_____

_____

_____

_____

_____

_____

_____

_____

_____

True inner joy is self –
created.
It does not depend on outer
circumstances.
A river is flowing in and
through you carrying the
message of joy.
This divine joy is the sole
purpose of life.

– SRI CHINMOY

What body sensations do you experience when you're feeling depressed (start from your head down to your feet)?

_____

_____

_____

_____

_____

_____

_____

_____

_____

_____

_____

_____

_____

_____

_____

_____

_____

If there is a future there is time for mending. Time to see your troubles coming to an ending. Life is never hopeless however great your sorrow.

If you're looking forward to a new tomorrow. If there is time for wishing then there is time for hoping–

When through doubt and darkness you are blindly groping.Though the heart be heavy and hurt you may be feeling. If there is time for praying there is time for healing. So if through your window there is a new day breaking.

Thank God for the promise, though mind and soul be aching, If with harvest over there is grain enough for gleaning. There is a new tomorrow and life still has meaning.

LIFE STILL HAS A MEANING -
RASKOME GABRIEL EYAEFE

What would you tell your best friend who was going through depression? What services and coping skills would you tell them to use?

_____

_____

_____

_____

_____

_____

_____

_____

_____

_____

_____

_____

_____

_____

_____

_____

_____

won't you celebrate with me
what i have shaped into
a kind of life? i had no model.
born in babylon
both nonwhite and woman
what did i see to be except myself?
i made it up
here on this bridge between
starshine and clay,
my one hand holding tight
my other hand; come celebrate
with me that everyday.

LET'S KEEP IN WON'T YOU
CELEBRATE WITH ME.

LUCILLE CLIFTONTOUCH

Have you experienced moments of crying without any triggers? How did you handle this situation?

_____

_____

_____

_____

_____

_____

_____

_____

_____

_____

_____

_____

_____

_____

_____

_____

_____

COPING WITH CRYING SPELLS

- Blinking and moving your eyes can help keep your tears at bay.

- Using distracting techniques to refocus your thoughts somewhere else.

- Deep breathing techniques to calm your emotional and thoughts.

- Using laugher to think about about something more positive.

- Communicating how you feel is an excellent way to deal with your emotions.

- Putting words to why you are crying is beneficial.

Explore your thoughts about your body image and how it's connected to your self-worth. What effect do you think the media has on your body image?

_____

_____

_____

_____

_____

_____

_____

_____

_____

_____

_____

_____

_____

_____

_____

_____

_____

_____

The most difficult thing
is the decision to act, the
rest is merely tenacity.
The fears are paper
tigers. You can do
anything you decide to
do. You can act to
change and control your
life; and the procedure,
the process is its own
reward.

-- Amelia Earhart

How do you think the world see's you?
vs
How do you see yourself?

_____

_____

_____

_____

_____

_____

_____

_____

_____

_____

_____

_____

_____

_____

_____

_____

_____

_____

Positive affirmations for a rough day.

- Today will be a wonderful day for me to remember.

- My thoughts are my reality so I will think of a glorious day.

- I fill my day with positivity and face the day with determination.

When you are feeling sad and low, what messages would you like to hear from your support system?

_____

_____

_____

_____

_____

_____

_____

_____

_____

_____

_____

_____

_____

_____

_____

_____

_____

_____

BE KIND TO YOUR OWN MIND:

WHEN IT WAKES YOU IN THE MIDDLE OF THE NIGHT,
(YOUR THOUGHTS AFRAID OF THEIR OWN SHADOWS;)
HOLD IT LIKE YOU HOLD A CHILD:
SOFTLY, YET WITH ALL YOUR MIGHT,
(TURN ITS TERROR INTO A FABLE;)
DON'T EVER BE ASHAMED TO LOVE YOURSELF.

Be kind to your own mind...-

Lenore

How can I be more compassionate to myself? Why is it worth trying?

_____

_____

_____

_____

_____

_____

_____

_____

_____

_____

_____

_____

_____

_____

_____

_____

Keep your

joy

♔ queen

Everyone's relationship with food is different; however, people who struggle with depression can overindulge or underindulge with foods. What is your relationship with food?

_____

_____

_____

_____

_____

_____

_____

_____

_____

_____

_____

_____

_____

_____

_____

_____

_____

IMPROVE YOUR MOOD WITH FOOD!

- Dark left greens
- Yogurt
- Salmon
- Eggs
- Blue berries
- Honey
- Oatmeal

Eat and be happy!

Commonly people with depression struggle from a lack of concentration. Do you struggle with a lack of focus? If so, how has it effected you? What have you done to regain concentration?

_____

_____

_____

_____

_____

_____

_____

_____

_____

_____

_____

_____

_____

_____

_____

_____

_____

"UNEXPRESSED EMOTIONS WILL NEVER DIE. THEY ARE BURIED ALIVE AND WILL COME FORTH LATER IN UGLIER WAYS."

— SIGMUND FREUD

What happens when you feel your depression has worsened do you: isolate yourself, push people away, become more irritable, lose motivation, or eat more? How has this behavior pattern affected you at work or in your personal relationships?

_____

_____

_____

_____

_____

_____

_____

_____

_____

_____

_____

_____

_____

_____

_____

_____

_____

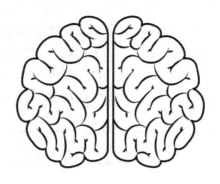

Train your brain to be more motivated:

- *CALL A FRIEND AND STAY SOCIAL.*

- *USE POSITIVE SELF-TALK. PICK A STRONG ASSERTIVE VOICE.*

- *REPEAT POSITIVE AFFIRMATIONS IN THE MIRROR.*

- *CREATE DAILY GOALS. REWARD YOURSELF FOR ACHIEVING YOUR GOALS.*

The hardest part of the day was _____ .
I will use these coping skills to help me move
forward, list them below.

_____

_____

_____

_____

_____

_____

_____

_____

_____

_____

_____

_____

_____

_____

_____

_____

_____

4 Ways to cope with Stress!

1

"Learn how to say "no." Know your limits and stick to them. Whether in your personal or professional life, taking on more than you can handle is a surefire recipe for stress. Distinguish between the "shoulds" and the "musts" and, when possible, say "no" to taking on too much."

2

"Avoid people who stress you out. If someone consistently causes stress in your life, limit the amount of time you spend with that person, or end the relationship."

3

"Pare down your to-do list. Analyze your schedule, responsibilities, and daily tasks. If you've got too much on your plate, drop tasks that aren't truly necessary to the bottom of the list or eliminate them entirely."

4

"Take control of your environment. If the evening news makes you anxious, turn off the TV. If traffic makes you tense, take a longer but less-traveled route. If going to the market is an unpleasant chore do your grocery shopping online."

When my life gets overwhelming, I find it easy when I _____ to cope with life stressors ?

_____

_____

_____

_____

_____

_____

_____

_____

_____

_____

_____

_____

_____

_____

_____

BE KIND TO YOURSELF

MY STORY ONLY BELONGS TO
ME, FACTS TO WHY I AM
UNIQUE.

I CHOOSE TO SEE THE LOVE
THAT THE WORLD HAS TO GIVE
NOT THE HATE.

I AM PROUD OF MY SKIN AND
WHAT MY BODY
WENT THOUGHT TO BE SO
MAGICAL.

I AM A GIFT TO MY CULTURE
AND TO MY COMMUNITY.

Do you compare yourself to others on social media if so how do you feel afterwards?

_____

_____

_____

_____

_____

_____

_____

_____

_____

_____

_____

_____

_____

_____

_____

_____

_____

Don't forget to tell yourself positive things daily!

You must love yourself internally to glow externally.

HANNAH BRONFMAN

Depression can stem from disheartening thoughts from your childhood. Can you describe a childhood memory when you were happy? Be specific recall the time of day, the weather, the person, and your emotions.

_____

_____

_____

_____

_____

_____

_____

_____

_____

_____

_____

_____

_____

_____

_____

_____

_____

The only limit to the height of your achievements is the reach of your dreams

AND YOUR WILLINGNESS

to work hard for them.

Michelle Obama

I have the most energy during what time of the day and doing what activites?

_____

_____

_____

_____

_____

_____

_____

_____

_____

_____

_____

_____

_____

_____

_____

_____

_____

Clean Up Room + Small Wins

If I'm feeling down and lack motivation, I try to knock out something small. For example, maybe I'll organize my nightstand drawer thats has gotten a little messy. This gives your brain a small win and some encouragement. Next, maybe I'll organize my closet. With another small win, I often feel generally happier and more motivated to keep working on other things. In general, I've found this can help lift me out of a depressive or anxious rut that I may be stuck in.

--Taylor Otwell

What small wins can you do when your feeling depressed? List small rewards for different settings in your life (home, work, and social settings).

_____

_____

_____

_____

_____

_____

_____

_____

_____

_____

_____

_____

_____

_____

_____

_____

_____

_____

_____

POSITIVE VISUALIZATION

LATELY I'VE FOUND IT HELPFUL
TO VISUALIZE THE KIND OF
PERSON I WANT TO BE. FOR
EXAMPLE, YOU CAN THINK
ABOUT PEOPLE FROM HISTORY
WHO ARE REALLY INSPIRING TO
YOU AND THE THINGS ABOUT
THEM YOU WOULD LIKE TO
EMULATE. OR, YOU COULD
VISUALIZE YOURSELF BEING THE
PATIENT, POSITIVE PERSON YOU
WANT TO BE. I'VE FOUND THIS
ALONE CAN INSPIRE MY MIND
AND GET ME RE-FOCUSED ON
HOW I WANT TO LIVE.

TAYLOR OTWELL.

If you had three magic wishes, what would they be? Do you think you will still be struggling with depression?

_____

_____

_____

_____

_____

_____

_____

_____

_____

_____

_____

_____

_____

_____

_____

_____

_____

_____

"Allow children to be happy in their own way, for what better way will they find?"

– Samuel Johnson

When feeling depressed, do you neglect your hygiene, if so what? What plan can you put in place to maintain a healthy hygiene regiment?

_____
_____
_____
_____
_____
_____
_____
_____
_____
_____
_____
_____
_____
_____
_____
_____
_____

"If I had my child to raise all over again, I'd build self-esteem first, and the house later. I'd finger-paint more, and point the finger less.

I would do less correcting and more connecting. I'd take my eyes off my watch, and watch with my eyes. I'd take more hikes and fly more kites.

I'd stop playing serious, and seriously play. I would run through more fields and gaze at more stars. I'd do more hugging and less tugging."

– Diane Loomans

Have you put on a fake smile to get through the day? What activities can you do to have a genuine smile?

_____

_____

_____

_____

_____

_____

_____

_____

_____

_____

_____

_____

_____

_____

_____

"When a child hits a child, we call it aggression. When a child hits an adult, we call it hostility. When an adult hits an adult, we call it assault. When an adult hits a child, we call it discipline."

- Haim G. Ginott

Do you check on your friends who
struggle with mental health illness?
How do you provide support for them?

_____
_____
_____
_____
_____
_____
_____
_____
_____
_____
_____
_____
_____
_____
_____
_____
_____
_____

THE MIND CHASES HAPPINESS.

THE HEART CREATES HAPPINESS.

THE SOUL IS HAPPINESS.

AND IT SPREADS HAPPINESS.

ALL-WHERE.

-SRI CHINMOY

Do you believe the future will be better then the past?

_____

_____

_____

_____

_____

_____

_____

_____

_____

_____

_____

_____

_____

_____

_____

LET US LIVE IN JOY, NOT
HATING THOSE WHO HATE
US.AMONG THOSE WHO HATE
US, WE LIVE FREE OF HATE.LET
US LIVE IN JOY,FREE FROM
DISEASE AMONG THOSE WHO
ARE DISEASED.AMONG THOSE
WHO ARE DISEASED, LET US
LIVE FREE OF DISEASE.LET US
LIVE IN JOY, FREE FROM GREED
AMONG THE GREEDY.AMONG
THOSE WHO ARE GREEDY, WE
LIVE FREE OF GREED.LET US LIVE
IN JOY, THOUGH WE POSSESS
NOTHING.LET US LIVE FEEDING
ON JOY, LIKE THE BRIGHT GODS.
-

THE BUDDHA

What do you have to get off your chest from today? Write your emotions down and leave them on the page.

_____

_____

_____

_____

_____

_____

_____

_____

_____

_____

_____

_____

_____

_____

_____

_____

_____

_____

_____

IT HOVERS BEHIND THE SCENES, PLACATED TEMPORARILY BY MEDICATION AND RENEWED ENERGY, WAITING TO SLITHER BACK IN, UNNOTICED BY OTHERS. IT SITS IN THE SPACE BEHIND YOUR EYES, MAKING ITS PRESENCE FELT EVEN IN THOSE MOMENTS WHEN OTHER, LIGHTER MATTERS ARE AT THE FOREFRONT OF YOUR MIND. IT TUGS AT YOU, KEEPING YOU FROM EVER BEING FULLY AT EASE. WORST OF ALL, IT HONORS NO SEASON AND RESPECTS NO CALENDAR; IT ARRIVES PRECISELY WHEN IT FEELS LIKE IT.

Martin Scorsese

How do you feel when you have to be alone?
What do you do to avoid being alone?-
No judgement

Questions to use when negative thoughts occur:

Reality testing

- What is my evidence for and against my thinking?

- Are my thoughts factual, or are they just my interpretations?

- Am I jumping to negative conclusions?

- How can I find out if my thoughts are actually true?

Alternative Explanations

- Are there any other ways that I could look at this situation?

- What else could this mean?

- If I were being positive, how would I perceive this situation.

By Ben Martin, Psy.D.

Questions to use when negative thoughts occur:

Alternative Explanations

- Is this situation as bad as I am making out to be?

- What is the worst thing that could happen?

- How likely is it?

- What is the best thing that could happen?

- What is most likely to happen?

- Is there anything good about this situation?

- Will this matter in five years time?

When you feel anxious, depressed or stressed-out your self-talk is likely to become extreme, you'll be more likely to expect the worst and focus on the most negative aspects of your situation. So, it's helpful to try and put things into their proper perspective.

By Ben Martin, Psy.D.

Questions to use when negative thoughts occur:

Using goal-directed thinking

- Is thinking this way helping me to feel good or to achieve my goals?

- What can I do that will help me solve the problem?

- Is there something I can learn from this situation, to help me do it better next time?

By Ben Martin, Psy.D.

Make a list of 30 things that make you smile.

_____

_____

_____

_____

_____

_____

_____

_____

_____

_____

_____

_____

_____

_____

_____

_____

_____

_____

_____

_____

_____

_____

_____

I choose to be thankful for the light of this new morning, and for renewed energy and strength to be who I know I can be.

Learning how to react vs. respond can help to manage feelings of irritability. Write down a moment that you demonstrated both.

_____

_____

_____

_____

_____

_____

_____

_____

_____

_____

_____

_____

_____

_____

_____

_____

_____

_____

I'M WILLING TO SEE BEAUTY WHERE OTHERS SEE NOTHING; I CAN LOOK BEYOND A ROCK AND UNCOVER THE DIAMOND. FOR THE ROCKS AND THE DIAMONDS, I AM THANKFUL, BECAUSE LIFE IS A RICH EXPERIENCE THAT INCLUDES EVERYTHING.

THE LAW OF ATTRACTION

What are some stigma's attached to depression? Do you believe you share these qualities? Have you ever told someone you are struggling with depression?

_____
_____
_____
_____
_____
_____
_____
_____
_____
_____
_____
_____
_____
_____
_____
_____
_____
_____
_____
_____
_____

I COMPLETELY ACCEPT HAPPINESS THAT WANTS TO APPEAR IN MY LIFE, AND I ACCEPT IT NOW IN THE BEST SPACE IN MY LIFE.

AND

I ACCEPT MY SORROWS AND MY BLESSINGS, SO I CAN CHANGE MY SORROWS INTO MY JOY.

What was the best decision you made recently? How did it improve your life?

_____

_____

_____

_____

_____

_____

_____

_____

_____

_____

_____

_____

_____

_____

_____

_____

_____

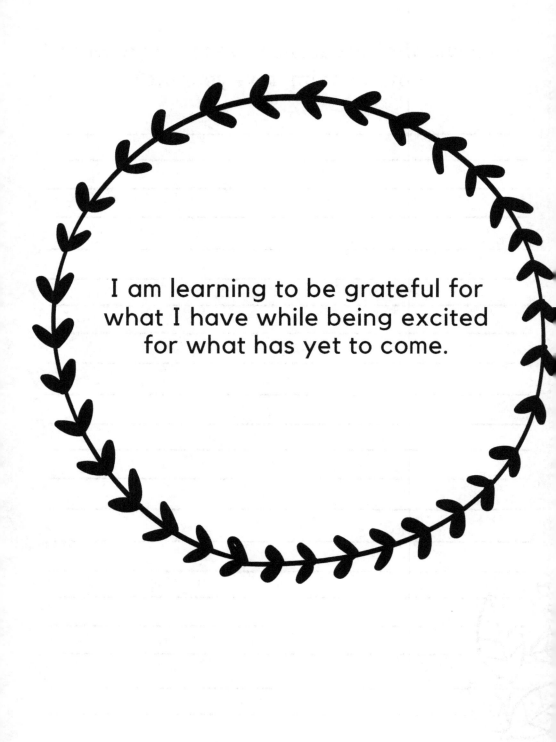

I am learning to be grateful for what I have while being excited for what has yet to come.

Our morals and values can change throughout life
experiences. They can change over time?
What are your current values and morals?

_____
_____
_____
_____
_____
_____
_____
_____
_____
_____
_____
_____
_____
_____
_____
_____
_____
_____
_____
_____

We don't develop courage by being happy every day. We develop it by surviving difficult times and challenging adversity.

BARBARA DE ANGELIS

Understanding your triggers can help manage your depression. Identify your thoughts that are linked to depression, think about relationships, work, and social settings?

_____
_____
_____
_____
_____
_____
_____
_____
_____
_____
_____
_____
_____
_____
_____
_____
_____
_____

By seizing the opportunities that disruption presents and leveraging hard times into greater success through outworking, out innovating, and outthinking everyone around you, this just might be the richest time of your life so far. -

Robin S. Sharma

What is something that you want someone to know about you, but you are too shy to share?

_____

_____

_____

_____

_____

_____

_____

_____

_____

_____

_____

_____

_____

_____

_____

_____

_____

_____

_____

When sore trials come upon us, it's time to deepen our faith in God, to work hard, and to serve others. Then He will heal our broken hearts. He will bestow upon us personal peace and comfort.

Russell M. Nelson

Make a list of things you need to let go in order to release your pain. Now rip the paper and start the process of healing.

Believe in yourself!
Have faith in your abilities!
Without a humble but
reasonable confidence in your
own powers you cannot be
successful or happy. –

Norman Vincent Peale

When I'm in physical or emotional pain what is the kindest thing I can do for myself?

Don't be afraid of your fears. They're not there to scare you. They're there to let you know that something is worth it.

C. JoyBell C.

Was there anything recently that made you laugh?

_____
_____
_____
_____
_____
_____
_____
_____
_____
_____
_____
_____
_____
_____
_____
_____

The most beautiful people we have known are those who known defeat, known suffering, known struggle, known loss, and have found their way out of the depths. These persons have an appreciation, a sensitivity, and an understanding of life that fills them with compassion, gentleness, and a deep loving concern. Beautiful people do not just happen. –

Elisabeth Kubler Ros

Who and what inspires you to think about yourself differently? How are they inspiring?

_____

_____

_____

_____

_____

_____

_____

_____

_____

_____

_____

_____

_____

_____

_____

HOPE IS BEING ABLE TO SEE THAT THERE IS LIGHT DESPITE ALL OF THE DARKNESS.

Desmond Tutu

What value can you add to your community that will lead to a positive change?

_____

_____

_____

_____

_____

_____

_____

_____

_____

_____

_____

_____

_____

_____

<u>Self-Care Tips:</u>

- Be kind to yourself.

- Show gratitude to others.

- Know your strengths.

- Exercise and stretch.

- Be a true friend.

- Stop comparing yourself to others.

How will you incorporate self-care techniques in your everyday life?

_____

_____

_____

_____

_____

_____

_____

_____

_____

_____

_____

_____

_____

_____

_____

_____

_____

_____

CAN YOU SING A SONG?
BY JOSEPH MORRIS

Can you sing a song to greet the sun,
Can you cheerily tackle the work to
be done,
Can you vision it finished when only
begun,
Can you sing a song? Can you sing a
song when the day's half through,
When even the thought of the rest
wearies you,
With so little done and so much to do,
Can you sing a song? Can you sing a
song at the close of the day,
When weary and tired, the work's put
away,
With the joy that it's done the best of
the pay,
Can you sing a song?

Write a letter to your body telling it how you feel?
This could be a love letter or letter of apology if you
have been critical of your body in the past.

_____

_____

_____

_____

_____

_____

_____

_____

_____

_____

_____

_____

_____

_____

_____

_____

_____

_____

Write about your day or week. Did something good or bad happen? Are you feeling happy or sad? Did you learn something new?

_____

_____

_____

_____

_____

_____

_____

_____

_____

_____

_____

_____

_____

_____

_____

_____

_____

_____

_____

_____

Social Media Detox

- Block all social media sites. This is for your computers, laptops, and tablets.

- Replace social media with another activity. It's not enough to just go cold turkey from social media.

- You need to fill that void with something else, otherwise you're just go way back to social media.

- I recommend learning new skills or giving back.

Make a list of things you would like to learn over the next year.

_____

_____

_____

_____

_____

_____

_____

_____

_____

_____

_____

_____

_____

_____

_____

_____

_____

_____

_____

_____

Social Media Detox

- Deactivate your accounts. This will serve as a hedge against you checking in on a whim, and it will also signal to your friends that you're on a detox.

- Uninstall all social media apps. This will eliminate all of those notifications and alerts that play such a crucial role in social media addiction. And you won't be as likely to pop one of those apps open in moments of boredom or stillness.

What brings you hope and joy when you are feeling down? What keeps you fighting to stay motivated?

_____
_____
_____
_____
_____
_____
_____
_____
_____
_____
_____
_____
_____
_____
_____
_____
_____
_____
_____

The golden way is to be friends with the world and to regard the whole human family as one.

MAHATMA GANDHI

What are some of your favorite songs to listen to when you are feeling sad? How do the lyrics affect your mood?

_____

_____

_____

_____

_____

_____

_____

_____

_____

_____

_____

_____

_____

_____

_____

_____

_____

_____

_____

When did you first experience feelings of sadness and who did you tell?

_____

_____

_____

_____

_____

_____

_____

_____

_____

_____

_____

_____

_____

_____

_____

_____

_____

_____

_____

_____

WHEN SOMEONE TELLS ME "NO," IT DOESN'T MEAN I CAN'T DO IT, IT SIMPLY MEANS I CAN'T DO IT WITH THEM.

Karen E. Quinones Miller

Did you practice positive visualization today?
If so, what did you visualize?
Remember to tap into all five senses.

_____

_____

_____

_____

_____

_____

_____

_____

_____

_____

_____

_____

_____

_____

_____

_____

_____

A LOT OF PEOPLE WILL IGNORE POSITIVE WORDS WHEN THEY ARE DOWN AND ACCEPT NEGATIVE WORDS. THOSE PEOPLE NEVER GET BETTER.

Travis J. Dahnke

What is your greatest hurdle you accomplished in a relationship? How did this situation help you to grow as a person?

_____

_____

_____

_____

_____

_____

_____

_____

_____

_____

_____

_____

_____

_____

_____

_____

_____

_____

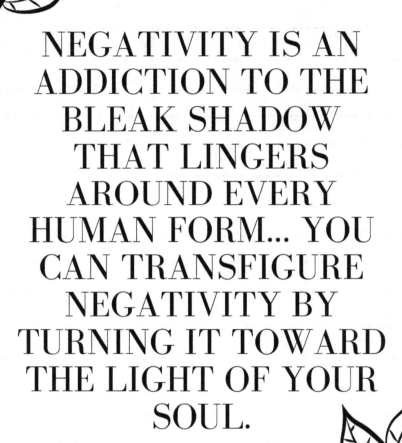

NEGATIVITY IS AN
ADDICTION TO THE
BLEAK SHADOW
THAT LINGERS
AROUND EVERY
HUMAN FORM... YOU
CAN TRANSFIGURE
NEGATIVITY BY
TURNING IT TOWARD
THE LIGHT OF YOUR
SOUL.

John O'Donohue

How do you handle conflicts within your relationships? How do they affect your emotions?

_____

_____

_____

_____

_____

_____

_____

_____

_____

_____

_____

_____

_____

_____

_____

_____

_____

Compassion is sometimes the fatal capacity for feeling what it is like to live inside somebody else's skin. It is the knowledge that there can never really be any peace and joy for me until there is peace and joy finally for you too.

FREDERICK BUECHNER

Describe the most impactful relationship you have (romantic or personal)?

_____

_____

_____

_____

_____

_____

_____

_____

_____

_____

_____

_____

_____

_____

_____

_____

_____

"WHEN SOMETHING BAD
HAPPENS YOU HAVE
THREE CHOICES. YOU
CAN EITHER LET IT
DEFINE YOU, LET IT
DESTROY YOU, OR YOU
CAN LET IT
STRENGTHEN YOU."

Dr. Seuss

What are you looking for in a partner? What are you willing to compromise to be with your partner?

_____

_____

_____

_____

_____

_____

_____

_____

_____

_____

_____

_____

_____

_____

_____

_____

_____

If we have no peace, it is because we have forgotten that we belong to each other.

MOTHER TERESA

What are some of your emotional and physical boundaries when it comes to a new relationship? Is this easy to articulate to your partner?

_____

_____

_____

_____

_____

_____

_____

_____

_____

_____

_____

_____

_____

_____

_____

_____

_____

_____

Darkness cannot drive out darkness; only light can do that. Hate cannot drive out hate; only love can do that.

Martin Luther King, Jr.

· · · · · · · · · ● ● ● ● ● ● ● ● ● ● · · · · · ·

Letting go of our past mistakes can increase feelings of depression. What do you do to acknowledge your mistakes? How has this affected your mental health ?

_____

_____

_____

_____

_____

_____

_____

_____

_____

_____

_____

_____

_____

_____

_____

_____

_____

_____

_____

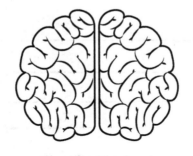

Introspection is always retrospection.

Sartre

Identify three negative statements you typically tell yourself. Then trace them back to who said them to you. Now be honest with yourself, are they true or false?

_____

_____

_____

_____

_____

_____

_____

_____

_____

_____

_____

_____

_____

_____

_____

_____

_____

_____

_____

_____

"I EAT EVERY TWO HOURS. I SLEEP FOR EIGHT HOURS. I HAVE LOTS OF WATER.

I pray to keep calm. Most importantly, I have a smile on my face."

Vidya Balan

List things that make you smile? Then write how often you are able to implement those activities.

_____

_____

_____

_____

_____

_____

_____

_____

_____

_____

_____

_____

_____

_____

_____

_____

_____

_____

_____

WE ARE MORE LIKELY TO DO THE THINGS WE SAY WE'RE GOING TO DO IF WE SCHEDULE TIME IN OUR CALENDARS TO DO THEM.
WE CAN ALSO MORE EASILY STAY ON TRACK IF WE GET ACCOUNTABILITY FROM OTHERS. SO IF YOU REALLY WANT TO BE HAPPIER, DON'T LET YOURSELF GET AWAY WITH BEING UNHAPPY.

TCHIKI DAVIS, PH.D.

Depression is a mental health illness that
can be managed with time. What symptoms
are you able to manage so far?

_____

_____

_____

_____

_____

_____

_____

_____

_____

_____

_____

_____

_____

_____

_____

_____

_____

_____

_____

"Laughter and smiling can actually trigger your brain to feel happier. When you're feeling down, listen to your favorite comedian, read a funny story, or watch a silly movie. It's healthy to laugh regularly. If you have a funny friend, make it a point to spend more time with them. They'll probably enjoy having someone to laugh with too."

Robert Porter

What are your most recent accomplishments?
What unique skills do you have?

_____

_____

_____

_____

_____

_____

_____

_____

_____

_____

_____

_____

_____

_____

_____

_____

_____

Even though happiness comes from within, all of us need other human relationships in our lives. Don't wait for your friends to contact you. Reach out and see how they are doing.

A friendship shouldn't be only about what you get from it. You will get more when you are also giving to the relationships you have with your friends, and that is why you need to know who you are first. You can only give yourself if you know what you have to give.

If you don't have a strong friend group, you may want to consider building one. Don't rush it."

By Robert Porter

When you feel like giving up what is the one thing
that keeps you from holding on? Where do you find
your strength?

_____

_____

_____

_____

_____

_____

_____

_____

_____

_____

_____

_____

_____

_____

_____

_____

_____

_____

"To develop enduring happiness in your life, you need to know what is important to you. It's about thinking about what kind of person you ultimately want to be. Goals may help you get there, but they are not the underlying values. Do you value family? Hard work? Art? Freedom? Fitness? Knowing who you want to help keep your mind focused on the important aspects of your life. Knowing that your values are the same, despite sad events, helps you keep going and find your happiness because you know who you are."

By Robert Porter

What does your spiritual practice teach you about finding hope? List scriptures that provide comfort and hope.

_____

_____

_____

_____

_____

_____

_____

_____

_____

_____

_____

_____

_____

_____

_____

_____

_____

_____

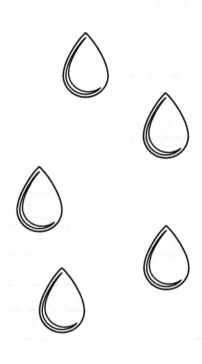

Tears are words that need to be written.

PAULO COELHO

Have you had counseling before? Describe your experience? What was the most impactful element about therapy?

_____

_____

_____

_____

_____

_____

_____

_____

_____

_____

_____

_____

_____

_____

_____

_____

_____

_____

_____

"Always find opportunities to make someone smile, and to offer random acts of kindness in everyday life."

Roy T. Bennett

What plan could you put in place to increase your sleep hours to get between 8-10 hours of sleep?

_____

_____

_____

_____

_____

_____

_____

_____

_____

_____

_____

_____

_____

_____

_____

_____

_____

_____

NOBODY DESERVES YOUR TEARS, *BUT* WHOEVER DESERVES THEM WILL NOT MAKE YOU CRY.

Gabriel Garcia Marquez

What are the factors that affect your sleep process?

_____

_____

_____

_____

_____

_____

_____

_____

_____

_____

_____

_____

_____

_____

_____

_____

"Never regret anything that made you smile."

MARK TWAIN

Who in your close circle reminds you of yourself and why?

_____

_____

_____

_____

_____

_____

_____

_____

_____

_____

_____

_____

_____

_____

_____

_____

Every human walks around with a certain kind of sadness.

THEY MAY NOT WEAR IT ON THEIR SLEEVES, BUT IT'S THERE IF YOU LOOK.

TARAJI P. HENSON

Staying connected to people is necessary for our emotional health, especially when feeling depressed. What social outings do you avoid when feeling depressed? How will you push yourself to stay engaged?

_____

_____

_____

_____

_____

_____

_____

_____

_____

_____

_____

_____

_____

_____

_____

_____

_____

_____

"Just follow your joy. Always. I think that if you do that, life will take you on the course that it's meant to take you."

Who in your life brings you joy and peace?
How does their energy affect your mood?

_____

_____

_____

_____

_____

_____

_____

_____

_____

_____

_____

_____

_____

_____

_____

_____

Inhale Love
Exhale Pain

Finding joy in small things is a great way to stay optimistic. Choose a "boring day" and find the joy in it?

_____

_____

_____

_____

_____

_____

_____

_____

_____

_____

_____

_____

_____

_____

_____

_____

HARD TIMES ARE MOMENTS OF REFLECTION.

Lailah Gifty

When you are feeling depressed, it can be hard to tell people how you feel. If you had to tell someone something, what would it be?

_____

_____

_____

_____

_____

_____

_____

_____

_____

_____

_____

_____

_____

_____

_____

_____

_____

_____

Never let your pain decide your future.

Erica Gilliams, LPC, ACS

Who in your life brings you joy and peace? How does their energy affect your mood?

_____

_____

_____

_____

_____

_____

_____

_____

_____

_____

_____

_____

_____

_____

_____

_____

_____

_____

"When we are kind to others, we feel better about ourselves. We can do nice things for others, be empathetic, or we can just treat each other with respect, communicating kindly rather than assuming the worst."

TCHIKI DAVIS, PH.D.

Think back to your last negative memory and process your emotions and the situation.

_____

_____

_____

_____

_____

_____

_____

_____

_____

_____

_____

_____

_____

_____

_____

_____

_____

"HARD TIMES MAY HAVE HELD YOU DOWN, BUT THEY WILL NOT LAST FOREVER. WHEN ALL IS SAID AND DONE, YOU WILL BE INCREASED."

Joel Osteen

Think of the last mistakes that you made. Did you blame yourself for the mistakes in your life? Are you able to learn from the mistakes?

_____

_____

_____

_____

_____

_____

_____

_____

_____

_____

_____

_____

_____

_____

_____

_____

_____

_____

Laugh
LO&VE

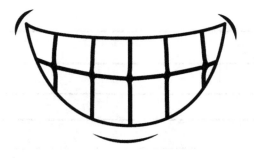

Goal setting is a life skill that changes as we evolve. What is your goal setting strategy? What obstacles hinders you from completing your goals.

_____

_____

_____

_____

_____

_____

_____

_____

_____

_____

_____

_____

_____

_____

_____

_____

_____

_____

YOU ARE NEVER TOO OLD TO REINVENT YOURSELF.

STEVE HARVEY

When we are feeling depressed, sometimes we can stay stuck on negative thoughts. How do you relieve yourself of your negative thoughts?

_____

_____

_____

_____

_____

_____

_____

_____

_____

_____

_____

_____

_____

_____

_____

_____

_____

_____

_____

_____

YOU NEVER KNOW HOW STRONG YOU ARE, UNTIL BEING STRONG IS YOUR ONLY CHOICE.

Bob Marley

I am grateful for………

"One thing to look at is your morals, ethics, and what gives you a sense of purpose in the world. Maybe, you have a nurturing spirit and want to work with children or have children of your own. It could be that you enjoy helping people, and there are a variety of avenues to pursue that through such as volunteer work, caregiving work, and work in the medical field. There are a couple of ways to get your brain pumping on this topic and start to think about what your purpose is and how to meet it in this lifetime."

By Sarah Fader

I am grateful to........

"A simple way to look at it is that happiness is something to work towards in your life; it's an end goal or destination. You can envision yourself in the state of happiness by achieving the goal of internal fulfillment; being content with who you are, what you have to offer the world, and how you can continue to grow. Joy, on the other hand, is a momentary effect or fleeting feeling. Happiness doesn't mean that you'll be happy all of the time; you'll still experience anger, grief, sadness, and a wide array of emotions, as we all do."

By Sarah Fader

What have you always dreamed about, but didn't believe you could achieve? Now, share this idea with a friend. Start a plan to put this dream into action.

_____

_____

_____

_____

_____

_____

_____

_____

_____

_____

_____

_____

_____

_____

_____

_____

_____

_____

"Facebook tends to have a negative effect on our happiness. By choosing to take breaks from Facebook — or changing the way we use social media — we can boost our happiness."

TCHIKI DAVIS, PH.D

How do you receive compliments? Do you say "Thank you" and believe it or minimized the compliments?

_____
_____
_____
_____
_____
_____
_____
_____
_____
_____
_____
_____
_____
_____
_____
_____
_____

LET'S FACE IT:
SOMETIMES WE ARE WHAT'S
MAKING US MISERABLE. WE
JUST CAN'T STOP THINKING
ABOUT HOW SO-AND-SO
WRONGED US, OR HOW OUR
LIFE DIDN'T TURN OUT AS WE
HOPED. NEGATIVE THOUGHT
PROCESSES
LIKE WORRYING, RUMINATIN
G, SELF-JUDGMENT,
AND FEARING REJECTION
JUST KEEP US MISERABLE
AND UNABLE TO MOVE
FORWARD. WHEN YOU FIND
YOURSELF THINKING
NEGATIVELY, PAUSE AND
REFOCUS YOUR THOUGHTS.
IN TIME, YOUR BRAIN WILL
BE ABLE TO DO THIS MORE
EASILY ON ITS OWN.

Tchiki Davis, Ph.D

List your best coping skills, and how do they help to manage your symptoms of depression.

_____

_____

_____

_____

_____

_____

_____

_____

_____

_____

_____

_____

_____

_____

_____

_____

_____

PAYING ATTENTION TO THE
GOOD, YOU CAN RISE ABOVE
IT AND BE MORE RESILIENT.
WHEN YOU FIND THE
GOOD, SAVOR THE MOMENT,
AND BRING IT WITH YOU TO
MAINTAIN HAPPINESS EVEN
DURING HARD TIMES.
OR TRY THINKING ABOUT A
TIME IN THE FUTURE WHEN
YOU'LL FEEL BETTER.

Tchiki Davis, Ph.D

What are ten things that irritate you? How do you manage those feelings?

_____

_____

_____

_____

_____

_____

_____

_____

_____

_____

_____

_____

_____

_____

_____

_____

_____

_____

Sometimes we want to escape. The world seems dark and scary, but by practicing mindfulness we experience more fully both the positive and the negative — we are more fully engaged in our lives.

Tchiki Davis, Ph.D

List your unhealthy thoughts and list how to challenge those thoughts?

_____

_____

_____

_____

_____

_____

_____

_____

_____

_____

_____

_____

_____

_____

_____

_____

_____

Sometimes we want to escape. The world seems dark and scary, but by practicing mindfulness we experience more fully both the positive and the negative — we are more fully engaged in our lives.

TCHIKI DAVIS, PH.D

What is a re-occurring compliment you receive? How does it make you feel to receive the same compliment?

_____

_____

_____

_____

_____

_____

_____

_____

_____

_____

_____

_____

_____

_____

_____

_____

_____

_____

Now that your eyes are open, make the sun jealous with your burning passion to start the day. Make the sun jealous or stay in bed.

MALAK EL HALABI

Write a letter to your happy self? Recall positive thoughts, activities, and your overall mood.

_____

_____

_____

_____

_____

_____

_____

_____

_____

_____

_____

_____

_____

_____

_____

_____

"Never apologize for being sensitive or emotional. Let this be a sign that you've got a big heart and aren't afraid to let others see it. Showing your emotions is a sign of strength."

B. NICOLE

If you had a superpower, what would it be? How would you help others? How would your life be different?

"JOY IS THE HOLY FIRE THAT KEEPS OUR PURPOSE WARM AND OUR INTELLIGENCE AGLOW."

Helen Keller

When was the last time you felt betrayed by someone? How were you able to cope with this situation? What did you learn about that person and your character while going through the situation?

_____

_____

_____

_____

_____

_____

_____

_____

_____

_____

_____

_____

_____

_____

_____

_____

_____

_____

Go ahead, tell me that I'm not good enough. Tell me I can't do it. Because I will show you over and over again that I can.-Unknown

Where and who do you feel the most physically and emotionally safe?

_____

_____

_____

_____

_____

_____

_____

_____

_____

_____

_____

_____

_____

_____

_____

_____

_____

Joy + Pain = Life

Erica Gilliams, LPC, ACS

What would you tell your future self?
Highlight yours high's and low's, give yourself
words of encouragement.

_____

_____

_____

_____

_____

_____

_____

_____

_____

_____

_____

_____

_____

_____

_____

_____

_____

_____

Community =Love
Family =Love
You =Love

Which music lyrics help you to feel better?

A queen and king is clothed with strength and dignity and laughs without fear of the future.

-unknown.

What is an activity that helps you to relieve feelings of depression that you can do at home without spending money? No more excuses.

"ALL THE ADVERSITY I'VE HAD IN MY LIFE, ALL MY TROUBLES AND OBSTACLES, HAVE STRENGTHENED ME.... YOU MAY NOT REALIZE IT WHEN IT HAPPENS, BUT A KICK IN THE TEETH MAY BE THE BEST THING IN THE WORLD FOR YOU."

WALT DISNEY

When was the last time you felt confident?
Describe what you were wearing, who were you
around, and what were you doing?

_____

_____

_____

_____

_____

_____

_____

_____

_____

_____

_____

_____

_____

_____

_____

_____

_____

_____

"There are two ways of exerting one's strength: one is pushing down, the other is pulling up."

BOOKER T. WASHINGTON

When was the last time you felt like you were not good enough?

_____

_____

_____

_____

_____

_____

_____

_____

_____

_____

_____

_____

_____

_____

_____

_____

_____

"I LIKE CRITICISM. IT MAKES YOU STRONG."

—LEBRON JAMES

When was the last time you stood up for yourself? What gives you the strength and courage to stand you for yourself this time.

_____

_____

_____

_____

_____

_____

_____

_____

_____

_____

_____

_____

_____

_____

_____

_____

_____

_____

YOU ARE MORE THAN YOUR DIAGNOSE!

ERICA GILLIAMS, LPC, ACS

What characteristics do you seek inorder to be more assertive? What will you do to gain these skills?

_____

_____

_____

_____

_____

_____

_____

_____

_____

_____

_____

_____

_____

_____

_____

May your days be

JOYFUL
& BRIGHT

Erica Gilliams, LPC, ACS

Describe the most
victorious moment in your life?

LOOK FOR THE

light from within.

Have you ever felt rejected? How did you react? Did this experience affect your self-worth?

_____

_____

_____

_____

_____

_____

_____

_____

_____

_____

_____

_____

_____

_____

_____

_____

_____

_____

Faith gives you an inner strength

AND A SENSE OF BALANCE AND PERSPECTIVE IN LIFE.

Gregory Peck

When you are at your lowest, who do you turn to for support? What kind of support does this person give you?

"IT'S MY EXPERIENCE THAT PEOPLE ARE A LOT MORE SYMPATHETIC IF THEY CAN SEE YOU HURTING, AND FOR THE MILLIONTH TIME IN MY LIFE I WISH FOR MEASLES OR SMALLPOX OR SOME OTHER EASILY UNDERSTOOD DISEASE JUST TO MAKE IT EASIER ON ME AND ALSO ON THEM."

• •

Jennifer Niven, All the Bright Places

Today, I felt good because I helped?

_____

_____

_____

_____

_____

_____

_____

_____

_____

_____

_____

_____

_____

_____

_____

_____

_____

_____

"TRY TO UNDERSTAND THE BLACKNESS, LETHARGY, HOPELESSNESS, AND LONELINESS THEY'RE GOING THROUGH. BE THERE FOR THEM WHEN THEY COME THROUGH THE OTHER SIDE. IT'S HARD TO BE A FRIEND TO SOMEONE WHO'S DEPRESSED, BUT IT IS ONE OF THE KINDEST, NOBLEST, AND BEST THINGS YOU WILL EVER DO."

STEPHEN FRY

Grief is a cycle and a ball of emotions. How has losing someone effected your grieving process?

_____

_____

_____

_____

_____

_____

_____

_____

_____

_____

_____

_____

_____

_____

_____

_____

_____

_____

The Five Stages of Grief

DENIAL- *IS THE FIRST OF THE FIVE STAGES OF GRIEF. IT HELPS US TO SURVIVE THE LOSS. IN THIS STAGE, THE WORLD BECOMES MEANINGLESS AND OVERWHELMING. LIFE MAKES NO SENSE.*

ANGER- *IS A NECESSARY STAGE OF THE HEALING PROCESS. BE WILLING TO FEEL YOUR ANGER, EVEN THOUGH IT MAY SEEM ENDLESS. THE MORE YOU TRULY FEEL IT, THE MORE IT WILL BEGIN TO DISSIPATE AND THE MORE YOU WILL HEAL.*

BARGAINING- *BEFORE A LOSS, IT SEEMS LIKE YOU WILL DO ANYTHING IF ONLY YOUR LOVED ONE WOULD BE SPARED. "PLEASE GOD, " YOU BARGAIN, "I WILL NEVER BE ANGRY AT MY WIFE AGAIN IF YOU'LL JUST LET HER LIVE." AFTER A LOSS, BARGAINING MAY TAKE THE FORM OF A TEMPORARY TRUCE.*

David Kesslerler

Grieving the loss of a loved one can be difficult. Journal all of your memories about them, positive and negativity.

_____

_____

_____

_____

_____

_____

_____

_____

_____

_____

_____

_____

_____

_____

_____

_____

_____

_____

_____

...stagings of greif

DEPRESSION -After bargaining, our attention moves squarely into the present. Empty feelings present themselves, and grief enters our lives on a deeper level, deeper than we ever imagined. This depressive stage feels as though it will last forever.

ACCEPTANCE- Acceptance is often confused with the notion of being "all right" or "OK" with what has happened. This is not the case. Most people don't ever feel OK or all right about the loss of a loved one. This stage is about accepting the reality that our loved one is physically gone and recognizing that this new reality is the permanent reality. We will never like this reality or make it OK, but eventually we accept it.

David Kesslerler

What is a particular saying your loved one used to say? Why was this saying so impactful ?

"WE NEVER LOSE OUR LOVED ONES. THEY ACCOMPANY US; THEY DON'T DISAPPEAR FROM OUR LIVES. WE ARE MERELY IN DIFFERENT ROOMS."

Paulo Coelho

What does your spiritual practice teach you about grief? Do those practices help you to cope with feelings of grief?

_____

_____

_____

_____

_____

_____

_____

_____

_____

_____

_____

_____

_____

_____

_____

_____

_____

_____

GRIEF IS SO HUMAN, AND IT HITS EVERYONE AT ONE POINT OR ANOTHER, AT LEAST, IN THEIR LIVES. IF YOU LOVE, YOU WILL GRIEVE, AND THAT'S JUST GIVEN."

Kay Redfield Jamison

When you are feeling down, write a special letter to your loved one? Be aware of your emotions and body sensations.

And when great souls die, after a period peace blooms, slowly and always irregularly. Spaces fill with a kind of soothing electric vibration. Our senses, restored, never to be the same, whisper to us. They existed. They existed. We can be. Be and be better. For they existed."

Maya Angelou

Use this space without the lines to express your feelings about grief. You can draw, add pictures, or write a poem.

WELLNESS KIT SUPPLIES

- Weighted blanket
- Lavender Tea
- Journal and pen
- Earbuds
- Soothing music

Today, I felt good because I helped?

In times of pain, when the future is too terrifying to contemplate and the past too painful to remember, I have learned to pay attention to right now. The precise moment I was in was always the only safe place for me.

Julia Cameron

What is a positive affirmation you tell yourself to feel more confident?

I WILL LOVE THE LIGHT
FOR IT SHOWS ME THE
WAY, YET I WILL
ENDURE THE DARKNESS
FOR IT SHOWS ME THE
STARS.

Og Mandino

What are your tell-tell signs that you are falling back into a depression? Focus on your thoughts and mood changes.

_____

_____

_____

_____

_____

_____

_____

_____

_____

_____

_____

_____

_____

_____

_____

_____

_____

_____

YOGA MOVES TO RELIEVE STRESS.

- Easy Pose
- Thunderbolt Pose
- Low PoseLatte
- Corpse Pose
- Wide-Legged Standing
- Standing Forward Bend

Movement can relieve feelings of depression and start to increase positive emotions. How will you move today?

_____

_____

_____

_____

_____

_____

_____

_____

_____

_____

_____

_____

_____

_____

_____

_____

_____

_____

THOSE WITH A GRATEFUL MINDSET TEND TO SEE THE MESSAGE IN THE MESS. AND EVEN THOUGH LIFE MAY KNOCK THEM DOWN, THE GRATEFUL FIND REASONS, IF EVEN SMALL ONES, TO GET UP.

Steve Maraboli

Depression can be passed on through genetics. Who in your family exhibits symptoms of depression? How do they cope with their symptoms?

_____

_____

_____

_____

_____

_____

_____

_____

_____

_____

_____

_____

_____

_____

Any fool can be happy. It takes a man with real heart to make beauty out of the stuff that makes us weep."

CLIVE BARKER

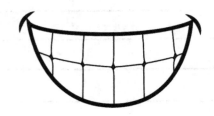

How do you handle uncertainty when feeling depressed?

POSTIVE AFFIRMATIONS:

My past maybe ugly, but my future is beautiful.

I am a work in progress.

Perfection is not necessary; I am at peace with imperfection.

I am worthy of peace, tranquility, and joy.

I am surrounded with love and support,

All is well in my life.

Everything is working out for my good. Out of this situation only good will come to me.

What are three words to live by to restore your balance and energy?

No man is an island, entire of itself; every man is a piece of the continent, a part of the main.

John Donne

Make a list of things you would like to learn over the next year.

_____

_____

_____

_____

_____

_____

_____

_____

_____

_____

_____

_____

_____

_____

_____

_____

_____

_____

_____

_____

NO PART OF THE
HUMAN
COMMUNITY CAN
LIVE ENTIRELY
ON ITS OWN
PLANET, WITH
ITS OWN LAWS
OF MOTION AND
CUT OFF FROM
THE REST OF
HUMANITY.

HUGO CHAVE

Write about how to ignore societal expectations when they clash with your belief system.